BLUEBIRDS

BLUEBIRDS
VERN THIESSEN

PLAYWRIGHTS CANADA PRESS
TORONTO

First edition: October 2022
Printed and bound in Canada by Rapido Books, Montreal

Jacket design by Gracia Lam

Playwrights Canada Press
202-269 Richmond St. W., Toronto, ON M5V 1X1
416.703.0013 | info@playwrightscanada.com | www.playwrightscanada.com

For professional or amateur production rights, please contact:
Michael Petrasek at Kensington Literary Representation
34 St. Andrew Street, Toronto, ON M5T 1K6
416.848.9648, kensingtonlit@rogers.com

LIBRARY AND ARCHIVES CANADA CATALOGUING IN PUBLICATION
Title: Bluebirds / Vern Thiessen.
Names: Thiessen, Vern, author.
Description: A play.
Identifiers: Canadiana (print) 20220279896 | Canadiana (ebook) 20220286000
  | ISBN 9780369103857 (softcover) | ISBN 9780369103871 (PDF)
  | ISBN 9780369103864 (HTML)
Classification: LCC PS8589.H4524 B58 2022 | DDC C812/.54—dc23

Playwrights Canada Press operates on land which is the ancestral home of the
Anishinaabe Nations (Ojibwe / Chippewa, Odawa, Potawatomi, Algonquin,
Saulteaux, Nipissing, and Mississauga), the Wendat, and the members of the
Haudenosaunee Confederacy (Mohawk, Oneida, Onondaga, Cayuga, Seneca,
and Tuscarora), as well as Metis and Inuit peoples. It always was and always will
be Indigenous land.

We acknowledge the support of the Canada Council for the Arts, the Ontario Arts
Council (OAC), Ontario Creates, and the Government of Canada for our publishing activities.

Canada Council   Conseil des arts
for the Arts   du Canada

ONTARIO ARTS COUNCIL
CONSEIL DES ARTS DE L'ONTARIO
an Ontario government agency
un organisme du gouvernement de l'Ontario

ONTARIO | ONTARIO
CREATES | CRÉATIF

for my sisters: Lori, Katie, & Ingrid

"I WOULDN'T HAVE MISSED IT FOR ANYTHING": MEET THE BLUEBIRDS

CYNTHIA TOMAN

A century has passed since the beginning of the First World War (FWW) when Canada first commissioned civilian nurses into the Canadian Army Medical Corps (CAMC). At the time it was considered inappropriate, even scandalous, for women to serve in active theatres of war. The level of carnage, however, made professional nursing care increasingly essential to military strategy. These military nurses, known by rank and title as Nursing Sisters, have quite a story to tell, but it remains relatively untold. They made up just one half of one per cent of the Canadian Expeditionary Force—only partially explaining their relative invisibility within official historical accounts. Their significance for the medical care of soldiers far outweighed their number and moves them from the periphery to the centre of military medical care provision during the war.

At least 600,000 Canadian soldiers served during the FWW with over 60,000 deaths. But, as one historian pointed out, "93 per cent of those who reached treatment [from the front lines] survived their wounds."[1] That was a remarkable outcome during an era prior to antibiotics with limited medical and surgical treatments. While official war histories bragged about teamwork within the military medical system, physicians frequently acknowledged that skilled nursing was the critical element in soldiers' care. A pathologist at Salonika (Greece), for instance, claimed, "There is no doubt in my mind now that the person who does the most

---

1 Desmond Morton, *When Your Number's Up: The Canadian Soldier in the First World War* (Toronto: Random House Canada, 1993), 181.

good in a hospital like ours, is the Nursing Sister. The majority of the men do not need a great deal of attention from the physician or surgeon, except now and then, but all the time the Sister is looking after them and it makes so much difference to them."[2] By the end of the war, the CAMC had admitted at least 761,635 soldiers.[3] Every one of them (in addition to thousands of Allied soldiers, untold numbers of prisoners of war, and civilians caught up in the action) passed through the hands of a nursing sister. The nursing sisters proved their worth in terms of outcomes for the soldiers while earning military honours and various accolades. Yet we know very little about them, their experiences, or their perspectives on the war. A small body of emerging historical research based on their letters, diaries, photographs, and oral histories sparked Vern Thiessen's interest.[4]

There is no one universal war story among the nursing sisters. At first glance, they appear remarkably similar in terms of demographics, but their first-person accounts are diverse. Each individual experienced the war within the context of her own personal needs, hopes, and dreams. Their stories also varied according to when they enlisted, how long they served, and where they were posted. Thiessen has listened closely to their accounts with the result that *Bluebirds* offers a glimpse of their war through three main characters who served on the Western Front.

Prior to the FWW (1914–1918) small groups of civilian nurses worked with the militia under special government contracts and later as volunteers with the British Army during the South African War (1899–1902). In 1904 the Canadian Army commissioned the first two permanent military nurses into its medical corps. They remained the only permanent force nurses until the FWW when 2,845 nursing sisters served, being the first and only commissioned women in the Allied forces for the duration

---

2   J. J. Mackenzie, *Number 4 Canadian Hospital: The Letters of Professor J. J. Mackenzie from the Salonika Front with a Memoir by His Wife, Kathleen Cuffe Mackenzie* (Toronto: Macmillan Company, 1933), 68.

3   Andrew Macphail, *The Medical Services: Official History of the Canadian Forces in the Great War, 1914–1919* (Ottawa: King's Printer, 1925), 6.

4   In addition to my own book, *Sister Soldiers of the Great War: The Nurses of the Canadian Army Medical Corps* (Vancouver and Toronto: UBC Press, 2016), see Susan Mann, *Margaret Macdonald: Imperial Daughter* (Montreal: McGill-Queen's University Press, 2005), and the included reading list.

of the war. As military officers with the relative rank of Lieutenant and official title of Lt./Nursing Sister, they received pay equal to men of the same rank—an unheard-of achievement for women of their time and far above their pay as civilian nurses. Matrons held the rank of Captain, and the Matron-in-Chief was a Major.

Canadian nurses were eager to enlist, their applications far exceeding established quota as the war dragged on. Like many of their brothers, fathers, and uncles, they wanted to participate in what was supposed to be "the last great war." Their mandate was to save the world (or at least their corner of the British Empire) through the care of sick and injured soldiers who could then return to the front lines. Their accounts ranged from vicarious participation in battlefield experiences, to angry repudiation of war, to deep weariness of war. Many expressed ambivalence and profound sadness about sending patients back to the front lines. As Nursing Sister (NS) Pearl Babbit wrote, "No one but those at the front and we who see the mangled bodies brought in still breathing, can have any idea of what is going on . . . It is too awful to write about."[5] Yet they did write—letters, postcards, and diaries. They also photographed their travels, friends, social activities, work units, and even occasionally patients.

The official criteria for appointment included being a British subject, single or widowed, graduation from a recognized three-year nurse-training program, high moral character and dignified deportment, physical fitness, and between twenty-one and thirty-eight years old on enlistment. While 13.4% of the CAMC nursing sisters were British-born, 83.2% were Canadian-born, primarily from English, Scottish, or Irish backgrounds. There were no women of colour or Indigenous women in the rank since Canadian training schools routinely excluded them from their programs. Although regulations stated that only single women and widows were eligible, records reveal exceptions to the rule. For example, the wives of two colonels were permitted to go overseas with their husbands as nursing sisters although they were not nurses and did no nursing. Nursing sisters were supposed to resign their commission upon marriage, and while most did, many others did not. One could truthfully be single on enlistment and then marry in secret, as long as pregnancy didn't

---

5   Pearl Babbit, letter of 8 June 1915, Library and Archives Canada [hereafter LAC], MG31G19, V. 5, G.W.L. Nicholson fonds.

interrupt things. The official criteria for appointment did not specify gender, but only women were appointed, although a small number of men were fully qualified trained nurses in Canada.

The average age on enlistment was 29.9 years, with quite a few individuals having adjusted their age downward to favour acceptance. The matron-in-chief, Major Margaret Macdonald, selected the nurses and gave preference to those with experience who had been hospital supervisors, or instructors within schools of nursing, or had extensive operating room experience. Older nurses were thought to be more mature and capable of maintaining discipline within large wards of potentially unruly men. Thus, age and the preference for extensive nursing experience positioned the nursing sisters more like "older sisters" in relation to the vast majority of their young (sometimes underage) patients, or "boys" as they called them. There were a few non-nurses in the rank in addition to the colonels' wives. One female physician/anaesthetist served as a nursing sister when she was not allowed to serve as a medical officer (an all-male rank). The rest served as housekeepers or clerical staff for the matron's office.

The CAMC nursing sisters served in Canada at recruiting centres and rehabilitation hospitals. They were posted to England and France (at large base hospitals along the French coast such as Le Havre, Rouen, Boulogne, Wimereux, Versailles, Dieppe, and Abbeville). Five hospital units were posted to the Mediterranean theatre with locations on Lemnos and Malta as well as at Alexandria (Egypt), Salonika (Thessaloniki, Greece), and Macedonia. Four nursing sisters served at the Anglo-Russian Hospital, established at Petrograd (Russia). Their postings moved them from country to country, hospital to hospital, and ward to ward contingent on where they were most needed at the time—often at short notice.

Geographical settings and battlefield contingencies determined the size and type of medical units. They ranged from small surgical field units near the front lines, to larger casualty clearing stations further back, to stationary hospitals located along lines of communication, to large general hospital units located further behind the lines with capacity for more than two thousand patients each. The nursing sisters were responsible for setting up these units, including operating theatres, wherever they went, often in tents or converted buildings such as churches or schools. There were also special hospital units for rehabilitation and psychiatric patients as well as hospital trains and ships for transporting the ill and wounded. Each setting presented unique challenges requiring nurses to improvise and adapt accordingly.

Military nursing work was often intermittent and shifted quickly from endless time spent waiting for battle action and the subsequent arrival of wounded patients, to times of intensive back-breaking work as convoys with hundreds (or even thousands) of wounded, gassed, and critically ill men arrived just hours after being injured. As NS Alice Isaacson wrote, "There is monotony *behind* the trenches as well as *in* the trenches. When the daily routine runs into months and years, it *may* become a bit of a *bore!*"[6] Work also had redeeming aspects, especially during big pushes, as NS Alfreda Attrill pointed out: "There was so much work to be done—we never had the time to stop and wonder; work saved us."[7]

Medical and surgical care included treatments for a variety of wounds and fractures, tetanus, gas gangrene, hemorrhage, trench fever, frostbite, blood poisoning, pneumonia, and mental illness. As poisonous gas filled the trenches, it damaged the lungs and eyes, causing suffocation and blindness with over a million casualties on the Western Front. Many soldiers suffered mental illness, referred to more or less interchangeably as "shell shock," "neurasthenia," or "hysteria," due to prolonged horrific stresses of the battlefield. They were often labelled as "cowards" and treatment ranged from court martial and execution, to electric shock, to sympathetic support and counselling later in the war. But the most fatal medical cause of death and debility in the CAMC was the 1918 influenza pandemic, which accounted for almost 46,000 cases and at least 776 deaths among patients and caregivers alike.

An unanticipated but significant part of caring for sick, injured, and dying soldiers involved writing letters to loved ones on their behalf. Matrons and nursing sisters took it upon themselves to write to soldiers' wives, parents, sisters, sweethearts, and even families of prisoners of war.

---

6   Alice Isaacson, diary, 1 Jan. 1918, LAC, R11203-0-1-E, Alice E. Isaacson fonds. Emphasis in original.

7   Lillian Gibbons, "An Album of Winnipeg Women: Miss A. J. Attrill," *Winnipeg Tribune*, no date, LAC, MG-31G-19, Gerald William Lingen Nicholson fonds.

They wrote on behalf of the living and the dead. They wrote for those who couldn't write for themselves either due to physical or psychological disabilities, or illiteracy. They wrote in situations where they felt a moral imperative to ease family suffering and grief regarding the injuries or loss of loved ones—offering an eyewitness account of their final hours and assuring relatives of decency and respect but mostly that their loved ones did not suffer alone.

Nursing sisters moved ever closer to the front lines, where they were increasingly vulnerable to injury and death themselves. In France they were exposed to poisonous gas. Many of those posted to the Mediterranean contracted malaria and suffered reoccurrences the rest of their lives. Still others suffered severe weight loss and debility from inadequate food supplies and sanitation.

The island of Lemnos, just off the coast of Gallipoli, was reputed to be the worst posting of the war—particularly bleak and barren. It was a sandy, rocky wasteland with few trees and no potable water. Navy vessels had to transport the precious water supply from Alexandria or distill it on board while in the harbour, which meant strict water rationing— only one quart per person per day for all purposes, including drinking and washing. Both patients and staff lived in tents with two coal-oil stoves per tent and straw mats for flooring. While heat, mosquitoes (and malaria), and flies made half of the year miserable, bitter cold made the other half miserable. Nursing sisters were under great strain there due to inconsistent and often inadequate food and water supplies. Two of them died of severe dysentery and are buried there.

Initially the CAMC went to lengths to assure the public that nursing sisters would only serve safely out of harm's way, far behind the front lines. But as the war stretched out, injuries increased in severity and soldiers became less expendable. Transportation to medical care further behind the lines delayed treatment and increased the death toll for hemorrhage and shock cases. The CAMC decided to move the nursing sisters forward, closer to the battlegrounds in order to save more lives. At least fifty-eight nursing sisters died as a result of enemy fire, disease, or drowning during the war.[8] Twenty-one of them died by direct enemy

---

8   Dianne Dodd, "Canadian Military Nurse Deaths in the First World War," *Canadian Bulletin of Medical History* 34, no. 2 (2017): 327–63.

action during the bombing of two hospitals in France and the sinking of the hospital ship *Llandovery Castle* off the coast of Ireland. Hospitals, hospital trains, and hospital ships displayed the Red Cross symbols and colours prominently to claim humanitarian protection under the Geneva Convention. But protective symbols failed to prevent hospital bombings at Étaples and Doullens on 19 and 29–30 May 1918 respectively. Neither did symbols prevent the *Llandovery Castle* from being torpedoed on 27 June 1918 during a return trip from Canada to England. In each incident, CAMC nursing sisters were wounded and killed.[9] The *Llandovery Castle* incident was ultimately prosecuted at Leipzig with three persons convicted as war criminals.

The CAMC nursing sisters went to war filled with idealism but very little awareness of what war or military nursing was. They expected some hardships and were determined to endure whatever came their way, but they had not anticipated their work to be dangerous or that some would die in the course of nursing duties. Many viewed the war as a great adventure with opportunities for overseas travel and a chance to renew their British roots. As NS Helen Petrie wrote, "It was wonderful . . . I'm so glad I was where I was so that I did not miss it."[10] Similarly NS Ruby Peterkin told her family that, "We are having the time of our lives and I wouldn't have missed it for anything."[11]

---

9   J. G. Adami, "The Enemy Air Raids Upon Canadian Hospitals, May 1918: A Report to the D.G.M.S. Canadian Contingencies," *Bulletin of the Canadian Army Medical Corps* 1, no. 5 (August 1918): 64–69; "The Sinking of H.M.H.S. 'Llandovery Castle'," *Bulletin of the Canadian Army Medical Corps* 1, no. 5 (August 1918): 69–73.

10   Helen Petrie, in *Letters from the Front: Being a Record of the Part Played by Officers of the Bank in the Great War, 1914–1919*, v. 1, ed. Charles Lyon Foster (Toronto: Canadian Bank of Commerce, 1919), 268–69.

11   Ruby Peterkin, letter of 3 December 1915, LAC, MG30-E160, Ruby Peterkin fonds.

FOR FURTHER READING (SECONDARY SOURCES)

Adami, J. G. "The Air Raid Upon No. 3 Canadian Stationary Hospital at Doullens, May 29–30, 1918." *Bulletin of the Canadian Army Medical Corps* (August 1918): 66–69.

———. "The Enemy Air Raids Upon Canadian Hospitals, May 1918." *Bulletin of the Canadian Army Medical Corps* (August 1918): 64–66.

———. "The Sinking of HMS 'Llandovery Castle.'" *Bulletin of the Canadian Army Medical Corps* (August 1918): 69–73.

Dewar, Katherine. *Called to Serve: Georgina Pope, Canadian Military Nursing Heroine.* Charlottetown, PEI: Island Studies Press, 2018.

Litalien, Michel. *Dans la tourmente: Deux hôpitaux militaries canadiens-français dans la France en guerre (1915–1919).* Outremont, Québec: Athéna éditions, 2003.

Mann, Susan. *Margaret Macdonald: Imperial Daughter.* Montreal: McGill-Queen's University Press, 2005.

Marshall, Debbie. *Give Your Other Vote to the Sister: A Woman's Journey into the Great War.* Calgary: University of Calgary Press, 2007.

Morin-Pelletier, Mélanie. *Briser les ailes de l'ange. Les infirmières militaires canadiennes (1914–1918).* Outremont, Québec: Athéna éditions, 2006.

Nicholson, G.W.L. *Canada's Nursing Sisters.* Toronto: Samuel Stevens Hakkert & Company, 1975.

Toman, Cynthia. "Eyewitness to Revolution: Canadian Military Nurses at Petrograd, 1915–17." In *One Hundred Years of Wartime Nursing Practices, 1854–1953,* edited by Jane Brooks and Christine E. Hallett, 122–43. Manchester: Manchester University Press, 2015.

— — —. " 'Help us, serve England': First World War Military Nursing and National Identities." *Canadian Bulletin of Medical History* 30, no. 1 (2013): 143–66.

— — —. " 'A Loyal Body of Empire Citizens': Military Nurses and Identity at Lemnos and Salonika, 1915–17." In *Place and Practice in Canadian Nursing History*, edited by Jayne Elliott, Meryn Stuart, and Cynthia Toman, 8–24. Vancouver: UBC Press, 2008.

— — —. *Sister Soldiers of the Great War: The Nurses of the Canadian Army Medical Corps.* Vancouver: UBC Press, 2016.

PUBLISHED MEMOIRS

Bruce, Constance. *Humour in Tragedy: Hospital Life behind 3 Fronts by a Canadian Nursing Sister.* London: Skeffington & Son, 1918.

Clint, Mabel B. *Our Bit: Memories of War Service by a Canadian Nursing-Sister.* Montreal: Barwick Limited, 1934.

Wilkinson, Maude. *Four Score and Ten: Memoirs of a Canadian Nurse.* Brampton, Ontario: Margaret M. Armstrong, 2003.

Wilson-Simmie, Katherine M. *Lights Out! A Canadian Nursing Sister's Tale.* Belleville, Ontario: Mika Publishing Company, 1981.

EDITED DIARIES

Gass, Clare. *The War Diary of Clare Gass, 1915–1918.* Edited by Susan Mann. Montreal: McGill-Queen's University Press, 2000.

Ridout, Peter H. H. *Nursing Sister Florence Alexandria Hunter [Ridout]: The Experiences of a Canadian Nursing Sister during the Great War.* Canada: Peter H. H. Ridout, 2006.

DIGITIZED EXHIBITS

Digitized biographies of six Nursing Sisters with some of their letters and photographs. https://www.bac-lac.gc.ca/eng/discover/military-heritage /first-world-war/canada-nursing-sisters/Pages/biographies.aspx.

Fowlds, Helen. Trent University Archives, Helen Maaryat Fonds, 69-001/1/1, boxes 1–2. http://digitalcollections.trentu.ca/exhibits/fowlds/.

Dr. Cynthia Toman, historian and retired professor from the University of Ottawa, taught in the School of Nursing with cross appointment to the Department of History. She was associate director and then director of the endowed Associated Medical Services Nursing History Research Unit. Her research focuses on the history of nursing and, specifically, the history of Canadian military nursing. Her major books, published by UBC Press, include Sister Soldiers of the Great War: The Nurses of the Canadian Army Medical Corps *(2016) and* An Officer and a Lady: Canadian Military Nursing and the Second World War *(2007). Awards include the Queen Elizabeth II Diamond Jubilee Medal, the Governor General's Gold Medal, the American Association for the History of Nursing's Teresa E. Christy Distinguished Writing Award, and the Canadian Historical Association's Hilda B. Neatby Prize. Toman was a guest curator for the 2005 "History of Canadian Nursing Exhibit" at the Canadian Museum of Civilization (now the Museum of History) and consultant to Historica Canada for a "Historical Minute" on First World War Canadian Nursing Sisters.*

This full-length version of *Bluebirds* was given its world premiere by Theatre New Brunswick on October 27, 2022, with the following cast and creative team:

Maggie: Kirsten Altar
Bab: Melanie LeBlanc
Christy: Sharisse LeBrun

Director: Natasha MacLellan
Stage Manager: Teagan Keith
Choreographer: Sarah Power
Costume Design: Sherry Kinnear
Set Design: Andrea Evans
Sound Design: Stewart Legere
Lighting Design: Chris Saad
Projections: Christian Ludwig Hansen

Production Manager: Nikki Vigneault
Head Carpenter: Jamie Atkinson
TNB General Manager: Joanna Bryson

CHARACTERS

Katherine Maud Macdonald (Christy)
Margaret Lowe (Maggie)
Gladys Mary Wake (Bab)

SETTING

The "real" setting is No. 1 Canadian General Hospital, near Étaples, France, 1918.

The theatrical setting is in the minds, memories, and hearts of the characters, which lives in the military cemeteries of Étaples and the nearby dunes overlooking the sea. There is no need for any attempt at realism. Their lives cross time and space.

PRODUCTION NOTES

Any race, age, gender identification, or physical ability can and should play these roles.

If possible, there should be movement, sound, and song. "Talking heads" should be avoided. All songs in the play are in the public domain and written during the time period of the Great War. They can be replaced or altered as a company sees fit. As much as possible, the songs, sounds, effects, alarms, whistles, etc., called for in the script should be created by the actors or live musicians.

Dawn.

A trinity *of women float up from memory's mist.*

They wear nightgowns.

They sing, their voices swinging in the air.

BAB: "Here we are . . .

MAGGIE: "Here we are . . .

CHRISTY: "Here we are again . . .

BAB: "There's Pat and Mac and Bonnie and Jack and Jo.

MAGGIE: "Never mind the weather . . .

CHRISTY: "Now we're all together . . .

ALL: "Hallo, hallo, here we are again."

* * *

CHRISTY: Dear Jack.

BAB: Dear Grandpa.

MAGGIE: Dear Annie.

If only you were here with me, feeling the salty spray of the English Channel on our cheeks.

It's a long way from Wolseley Avenue in Winnipeg to the Strait of Dover, I'm tellin' ya. And I've done my share of roamin', as you know. Five years old if a day, and we move across the world to Manitoba. And I thought Scotland was cold!

I'm thinking of the time, on a break at nursing school, staring down at the Assiniboine, its slow shallow waters as tedious as the city itself, and you sayin':

BAB: "Margaret Lowe, would you like to go on an adventure?"

MAGGIE: And that Sunday, our one day off, you pack us lunch and we head to the CPR station. We clamber onto the train, jammed with people: carpenters and lawyers, beautiful young ladies and old women, laughing children and barking dogs . . . and seventy minutes north, there we are.

Winnipeg Beach. Another world. Soft white sand and a burning hot sun. Warm summer water and a gentle cool breeze. We wade in, our bloomers up to our necks.

There we are. Floating. Healed for a moment from our . . . restlessness.

We take the evening train back, my sun-soaked head asleep on your shoulder. An' back home, a letter waitin' for me. Special delivery.

CHRISTY: "Nurse Margaret Lowe. You shall report for overseas duty immediately."

MAGGIE: The war calls.

BAB: (*correcting*) "Duty calls . . . "

MAGGIE: You take me to the train station again.

CHRISTY: "Good luck, Maggie. Write to me?"

MAGGIE: And then it's across the country to Halifax and across the pond to England. And now, here I am, Dover behind me and Calais on the horizon.

Och, Annie. Just when one world was opening up, I'm called to another. I'll write you every day.

* * *

BAB: Dearest Grandpa. You'd love this. On a transport, chopping across the grey waves of the Atlantic, another world on the horizon. The things you'd teach me! Like when I was a kid:

Showing me how to dig deep for red rock crabs and purple sea stars. Teaching me to swim to the wooden buoys and back. Schooling me to catch fish straight from the ocean and fry them up right there on the beach. Training me to sail your sloop around the cove. And as we tack our way into the wind, leaving the safe shore behind, you tell me tales of the sea.

(excited) How the Salish could tame these treacherous waters in their red cedar canoes. How the reefs of Juan de Fuca became the graves of sailors on the *Tonquin*, the *Melfort*, the *Valencia*. How, at night, when the lighthouse at Trial Islands sweeps past the dark waters, you can still see the ghosts of men waving for help.

Teaching me to fear the water, but love it too.

MAGGIE: "The sea will keep your secrets, Bab. Speak to it, and it will always set you right."

BAB: Three years ago, they find your sloop, abandoned, on Thetis Island. And no sign of you. What happened to you, Grandpa? A secret only the sea knows.

MAGGIE: People die, Bab. But stories never drown.

BAB: Nursing school in Victoria. Graduate with honours. There I am, cap and gown, standing on Macaulay Point in Esquimalt. Staring out at the Olympic range in the distance, and only a great invisible border between. What now? And I hear you say:

CHRISTY: "The sea doesn't care about borders, Bab. That's an idea created by men. Go around the cove, Bab. There's always something new to discover."

BAB: Now here I am. On my way to France watching all those waves smiling back at me, I'm going to be like you, Grandpa. I'm going to discover things past the cove. I'm going to collect stories. And tell them to *my* grandchildren.

* * *

CHRISTY: Dearest Jack. It's only been a few days since we saw each other, but it feels like . . .

CHRISTY vomits over the side of an imaginary ship.

It has only just occurred to me this is my first time on a ship. I've never crossed Lake Erie, let alone the Atlantic. Nineteen nurses on board and me the only one who gets siiii—

She retches.

When I think of rough water, it's near Elora Gorge, up the Grand River. Mother'd never allow us on that white water:

MAGGIE: "Stay away from there. Too rough and dangerous for a girl."

CHRISTY: Would have been nice practise, Mother.

She calms.

The only thing that calms my topsy-turvy stomach is you, Jack.

We've known each other a long time. You pulling my ponytail in grade school. Me kicking your shins then wiping away your tears. Us kissing for the first time at sixteen. After high school, you working at the telephone factory in Brantford and me at nursing school.

MAGGIE: "There's a war, Christy! We can't miss a war!"

CHRISTY: We enlist the same day. And two days later, you kiss me farewell.

MAGGIE: "It'll be an adventure! I'll be right behind you."

CHRISTY: Mother sees me off. Hands me a Bible:

BAB: "Keep God close, Christy, and you'll always be safe."

CHRISTY: Train to Toronto, then to Halifax, then to London, and now . . .

CHRISTY is nauseous.

(calming herself) "Love is patient, love is kind. It does not envy, it does not boast, it is not proud."

It passes.

Whadya know, Jack? A good Bible verse calms the stomach. This *will* be an adventure!

*** *** ***

They are now fully in light and fully alive. They sing, joyously.

MAGGIE: "Never mind the weather . . .

CHRISTY: "Now we're all together . . .

ALL: "Hallo, hallo, here we are again."

CHRISTY and BAB laugh with excitement.

*** *** ***

BAB: *(as a recruiter)* Ladies. I said, LADIES.

The other two settle.

You are being considered for appointment to the Canadian Army Medical Corps to serve overseas. Do you understand?

CHRISTY & MAGGIE: Yes, ma'am!

BAB: But you must pass the following criteria. One: being a British subject.

CHRISTY & MAGGIE: Check.

BAB: Two: graduation from a Canadian-recognized three-year nurse training program.

CHRISTY & MAGGIE: Check.

BAB: Three: high moral character.

CHRISTY & MAGGIE: Check.

CHRISTY: *(to MAGGIE)* I hope.

BAB: Four: physical fitness.

CHRISTY & MAGGIE: Check.

CHRISTY & MAGGIE: Five: between twenty-one and thirty-eight years of age on enlistment.

CHRISTY & MAGGIE: Check.

BAB: Six: not married.

MAGGIE: Check.

CHRISTY: . . .

BAB: I said, *not married.*

CHRISTY: Oh! Check!

BAB: Your mandate is to care for sick and injured soldiers, with the military objective of returning them to the front lines as soon as possible. Is that clear?

CHRISTY & MAGGIE: Yes, ma'am.

BAB: You are now "Taken on Strength."

CHRISTY: What's that mean?

MAGGIE: You're on active duty.

CHRISTY: *(confused)* Huh?

MAGGIE: *(rubbing her finger and thumb)* On the payroll!?

CHRISTY: OH!

* * *

MAGGIE: *(as a matron)* Sisters: your uniforms.

Their uniforms appear.

Perhaps they arrive from the heavens.

Perhaps they have been floating on the stage the entire time.

No matter how, their entrance is magical.

They are a stunningly beautiful shade of blue.

These are the public face of our institution. They communicate the values we hold:

CHRISTY: Virtue.

BAB: Authority.

CHRISTY: Expertise.

BAB: Responsibility.

CHRISTY: Obedience.

They put the uniforms on over their nightgowns.

BAB: Every nursing sister shall have:

MAGGIE: Four working dresses of light blue.

CHRISTY: Fourteen gilt buttons.

BAB: Rank badges—two stars on each shoulder.

MAGGIE: Twelve full aprons with square bibs.

CHRISTY: Crossed straps and square pocket on each side.

BAB: Eight collars—

MAGGIE: Eton style.

CHRISTY: And cuffs—

BAB: Bishop pattern.

MAGGIE: Eight muslin veils.

MAGGIE: Tan leather belt.

CHRISTY: Laced tan boots.

BAB: Tan stockings.

MAGGIE: Tan gloves.

CHRISTY: Military hat and coat.

BAB: Sweater.

CHRISTY: Umbrella.

BAB: And best of all?

ALL: *(surprised and delighted)* No corsets?!

CHRISTY: *(as a man)* It would restrict movement.

BAB: *(as a man)* Do you know how much a corset costs to make?

ALL: *(as men)* We're in a WAR, dammit!

MAGGIE: *(sardonicly)* Only when it makes sense to men does change happen for a woman.

BAB: We'll change things from now on.

CHRISTY: I don't care. Just look at this . . . BRASSIERE!

CHRISTY holds one up.

MAGGIE: *(as a matron)* You are now officially part of the CAMC. As professional, trained nurses, we have been given the rank of lieutenant. You are Canadian Nursing Sisters. But the boys will call you . . .

CHRISTY: Bluebirds.

BAB: Bluebirds.

* * *

They sing:

BAB: "Since the world began it's been up to man

CHRISTY: "To go forth and fight the foe

MAGGIE: "And with aching heart to sadly part
From the ones that he loved so

BAB: "Now it may seem strange to suggest a change

CHRISTY: "But it seems all right to me

MAGGIE: "And the Canuck maid who is ne'er afraid
I am sure with me'll agree

ALL: "Why can't a girl be a soldier
Just the same as her sweetheart brave

CHRISTY: "In the days of old women fair and bold
Their lives for their country gave

MAGGIE: "Give her a nice hat with feathers
A jacket and a dress of blue

BAB: "And she'll carry a gun good as any mother's son

ALL: "And she'll make a good soldier too

CHRISTY: "She'll carry a gun good as any mother's son

ALL: "And she'll make a good soldier too."

* * *

MAGGIE: Hello.

CHRISTY: Hello.

BAB: Hi.

MAGGIE: Ever been in a theatre of war?

BAB: I've only been in France since this morning.

CHRISTY: I've never been to any theatre. My mother doesn't approve.

MAGGIE and BAB look at CHRISTY, charmed.

A distant noise.

BAB: Is that thunder?

MAGGIE: The front. A few hours up the rail line.

BAB: Those are . . . guns? From that far away?

MAGGIE: And soon you'll see what those guns can do. I'm Maggie.

BAB: Bab. Scotland?

MAGGIE: Winnipeg now. You?

BAB: Victoria.

MAGGIE: You?

CHRISTY: I'm from London.

They look at her.

Ontario.

They look at her.

Brantford, really.

MAGGIE: Welcome to Canadian Field Hospital #1. Here's what you need to know: Stretcher bearers at the front collect injured to go to the clearing stations, then to dressing stations, then via the train line to us. After us, we send them back home, to England, for recovery, or back into the line. Make sense?

BAB: Yes.

CHRISTY: I think so.

MAGGIE: Over there's the mess where we eat, over there's the quarters where we sleep, over there's the wards where we work, and over there's a makeshift chapel where Sunday services are held.

CHRISTY: Oh, my mother will like that.

MAGGIE: Religion?

CHRISTY: Church of England. You?

MAGGIE: The Kirk.

CHRISTY: ?

MAGGIE: Scots Presbyterian. You?

BAB: Whatever makes sense in the moment.

* * *

MAGGIE: Here are your duties and authorities:

BAB: Forty-two instructions?!

CHRISTY: Lord have mercy!

MAGGIE: Manage all of the day-to-day details of the wards:

CHRISTY: Order food.

BAB: Take care of dietary intake for ill and wounded patients.

CHRISTY: Organize the supplies and equipment.

MAGGIE: Ensure all ward equipment and beds are completely antiseptic before new patients are admitted.

CHRISTY: Keep a daily record . . .

BAB: And a weekly one!

ALL: On each patient!

BAB: Write up doctors' orders on charts.

CHRISTY: Draw supplies as needed.

BAB: Supervise the loading and unloading of ambulance trains.

CHRISTY: Arrange transfer of patients back to England.

MAGGIE: In addition . . .

CHRISTY: There's more?

MAGGIE: Supervise the orderlies.

BAB: Account for all drugs as well as organize the wines and spirits.

CHRISTY: Notify the chaplain of patients' religious preferences . . .

MAGGIE: Prepare the dead.

CHRISTY: The dead?

BAB: The dead.

MAGGIE: Aye. The dead.

We are expected to endure all conditions. Our wards are our battle-fields. We will soldier on through whatever conditions we encounter. Because . . .

We ARE soldiers. And THAT is why we have these two stars on our shoulders.

* * *

CHRISTY: Dear Jack.

BAB: Dearest Grandpa.

MAGGIE: Dear Annie.

BAB: Odd, but it feels almost comfortable here.

CHRISTY: It's like a summer camp, but in war time.

MAGGIE: We Canadians are seen as hardy.

CHRISTY: Adventurous.

BAB: Accustomed to "primitive" conditions.

CHRISTY: Efficient in making due.

MAGGIE: We are paid two dollars per day and a mess allowance of one dollar per day. AND a field allowance while overseas of sixty cents per day. AND any travel allowances.

CHRISTY: Our money is paid directly . . .

BAB: Like manna!

CHRISTY: . . . into our bank account!

BAB: Meanwhile the English nurses receive a trifle: forty pounds a YEAR. And no rank. Oh, how they resent us.

MAGGIE: They call us:

CHRISTY: "Millionaire Colonials."

MAGGIE: "From the Dominions."

BAB: "Common Canadians."

MAGGIE: And, Annie, their poor uniforms!

CHRISTY: (sadly) So ugly.

MAGGIE: A grey chambray cape . . .

CHRISTY: With godawful red edging.

MAGGIE: They look at us, with our pay, rank, and beautiful blue uniforms . . .

CHRISTY: And they are green with envy.

BAB: Unlike the English, we get to eat with the officers!

MAGGIE: At first, the officers weren't so sure about having a mess for men and women together.

CHRISTY: (as a man) Not appropriate.

MAGGIE: *(as a man)* Should eat with your own.

BAB: *(as a man)* Could lead to . . . conversation!

MAGGIE: Funny how a few conversations with a woman always brings them round in the end.

BAB: I hope you don't think I am bragging, Grandpa, but the truth is:

MAGGIE: Their nursing is punk.

BAB: Completely untrained.

CHRISTY: It's shocking, Jack. They have no experience beyond bandaging a skinned knee. So look for a Canadian Bluebird if you ever get injured, God forbid.

ALL: I've been assigned a tent with two fellow sisters.

CHRISTY: Margaret Lowe.

MAGGIE: Call me Maggie.

CHRISTY: She seems very mature.

BAB: She's been here longer.

CHRISTY: She's taught us a lot.

BAB: A bit crusty.

CHRISTY: Like a mother, but the one you always wanted and didn't get.

MAGGIE: And there's Katherine Maud Macdonald.

CHRISTY: Call me Christy.

MAGGIE: Such a sweet thing.

BAB: Like a kitten playing with thread.

MAGGIE: And yet, inside more like—

BAB: A cat pouncing on a bird.

CHRISTY: Gladys Mary Wake.

BAB: Everyone calls me Bab.

CHRISTY: Bab scares me sometimes.

MAGGIE: Determined.

CHRISTY: Tough as nails.

MAGGIE: But fair.

CHRISTY: Like a battle commander, if such a thing could ever happen.

ALL: We all get along very well.

***

CHRISTY: Who do you write to, Maggie?

MAGGIE: A friend. We . . . roomed together in nursing school.

CHRISTY: *(oblivious)* That's nice. You write to her every day?

MAGGIE: Yes. I mean, sometimes.

BAB: Who do you write to, Christy?

CHRISTY: My, uh, a boy.

BAB: How you know him?

CHRISTY: Back home.

BAB: Where's he at?

CHRISTY: Stationed in England.

BAB: Will you see him on leave?

CHRISTY: If I can.

BAB: Plenty of handsome men here.

CHRISTY: No, I'd never . . .

BAB: You're young. You got time.

CHRISTY: It's not that, it's —

BAB: What?

MAGGIE: *(to BAB)* What are you doing there, Bab?

BAB: Writing my grandpa.

MAGGIE: In a diary?

BAB: He's dead.

CHRISTY: *(confused)* Ah!

BAB: He liked telling stories. It feels better than writing "Dear Diary."

CHRISTY: Besides, diaries aren't allowed.

BAB: Bah!

MAGGIE: *(joking)* Might fall into the hands of the Huns.

CHRISTY: God forbid they find out what we ate for breakfast!

MAGGIE: *(excitedly)* Is that a camera?

BAB: Vest Pocket Kodak. It was my grandpa's.

CHRISTY: Only officers are allowed cameras!

MAGGIE: *(joking) Kamera!? Verboten!*

CHRISTY: I thought you were Scottish?

BAB: Smile, sisters!

CHRISTY: Wait, I'm not ready!

BAB: We want to remember these times, right?

CHRISTY: Use my good side!

MAGGIE: See if you get us all in!

BAB: Pose for posterity!

They pose.

As close to a selfie as they can manage.

Snap.

A whistle.

They freeze.

What's that?

The whistle again.

MAGGIE: The signal.

CHRISTY: For what?

MAGGIE: They're coming.

BAB: The soldiers?

MAGGIE: The boys. The wounded.

BAB: *(steeling herself)* All right then.

CHRISTY: Oh God. What if I, what if I can't—?

MAGGIE: No time for that now. This is why we're here.

* * *

MAGGIE: It's a great healing machine, Annie.

BAB: So many, Grandpa.

CHRISTY: And so fast, Jack.

MAGGIE: Ambulances rush from the train station.

CHRISTY: Unload the stretchers.

MAGGIE: Pass them by the admitting officer.

BAB: Immediate Care
Likely to Live
Will Not Survive.

> CHRISTY *repeats as:*

CHRISTY: Lying
Sitting
Able to Walk.

> MAGGIE *repeats as:*

MAGGIE: Tetanus
Infection
Gangrene.

Tie a field medical card to the uniform, like this. Write down the following:

Type of wound:

BAB: Shot through the chest.

CHRISTY: Arm blown off.

BAB: Spine case—paralyzed.

MAGGIE: Prioritize treatment:

BAB: Clean dirt from the wound.

CHRISTY: Antiseptic to kill bacteria.

BAB: Surgery.

MAGGIE: Follow up.

BAB: Reduce pain.

CHRISTY: Replace dressing.

BAB: Replenish fluids.

MAGGIE: Keep moving.

BAB: But—

MAGGIE: Faster.

CHRISTY: I can't—

MAGGIE: You can. Go!

BAB: In the operating room I remove shrapnel from wounds. Control bleeding. Help repair fractures. Amputate limbs. I've never seen so much, so much . . . *(overwhelmed)*

MAGGIE: *(kindly)* Focus, sister.

BAB: Give tetanus shot. Check for infection, gangrene, hemorrhage.

MAGGIE: Sister, call the orderlies to carry up stretchers to the ward.

CHRISTY: I do. They undress and bathe the patients. They put each article of clothing on the helpless boys.

MAGGIE: Serve the food, sister.

CHRISTY: I raise a spoon to their swollen lips.

MAGGIE: Make a report for each soldier:

CHRISTY: Name?
Regiment?
Religion?
Any relations?

MAGGIE: Make a list of wounds. Then send it all to the War Office.

CHRISTY: Yes, sister.

MAGGIE: Keep moving, sisters.

BAB: Non-stop.

CHRISTY: Twenty-five hours straight.

MAGGIE: Last thing: make lists of the dead.

They stop. Look at one another.

CHRISTY: The dead?

BAB: The dead.

MAGGIE: Aye. The dead.

BAB: So many, Grandpa. So many.

CHRISTY: Jack, if you were to stay stationed in England . . . that wouldn't be such a bad thing. You know?

* * *

They hum a soft, soothing song:

"A Soldier's Mother's Lullaby."

MAGGIE: Night duty.

CHRISTY: I like the nights. It's relatively quiet. You can hear the passing purr of the patrol ships from the ocean, like kittens searching for a bowl of cream. The boys asleep.

BAB: Not me. It's the time I feel most alone. Like I'm drowning in a dark ocean.

CHRISTY: The searchlights sweep the sky, light up the wards. It's pretty, in its own way.

BAB: The rows of ghastly faces, woken by nightmares. More like spirits than men. Like the ghosts of shipwrecked sailors.

MAGGIE: Beauty and horror, together in one room.

The alarm—again. As at the start.

The voices we heard earlier—but softer and more haunting.

Shadows of planes, like birds, cross their faces.

CHRISTY: Two a.m.

BAB: High above us.

CHRISTY: Enemy planes.

BAB: *(mimicking the drone of the airplanes)* Muuuh, muuuh, muuuh—

MAGGIE: Lights out, please!

BAB: Pitch black. I hate it so.

CHRISTY: Huns.

MAGGIE: The Germans.

BAB: Threatening. Muuuh, muuuh, muuuh—

MAGGIE: All night.

BAB: This is as close to the front as I want to be, thank you.

CHRISTY: Never really thought about it before now.

BAB: What?

CHRISTY: Dying. Here. For this.

MAGGIE: Shush now.

CHRISTY: "The Lord is my salvation—whom shall I fear?"

BAB: Muuuh, muuuh, muuuh—

CHRISTY: "The Lord is my stronghold—of whom shall I be afraid?"

BAB: Muuuh, muuuh, muuuh—

MAGGIE: We wait.

CHRISTY: And wait.

BAB: And wait.

Silence.

CHRISTY: And then . . .

The all-clear is sounded.

MAGGIE: All clear! You all right?

BAB: I suppose. You?

CHRISTY: *(relieved)* Yes.

MAGGIE: Congratulations, sisters. You survived your first air-raid warning.

CHRISTY: But no rest.

BAB: No.

MAGGIE: A convoy of wounded soldiers. Three thousand Canadians. Travelling under the cover of darkness. Move!

BAB: Prepare current patients for evacuation by eight a.m.

CHRISTY: Wake up the men. Drag them out.

BAB: Poor boys.

MAGGIE: Here come the new ones.

BAB: Immediate Care
Likely to Live
Will Not Survive.

CHRISTY *repeats as:*

CHRISTY: Lying
Sitting
Able to Walk.

MAGGIE *repeats as:*

MAGGIE: Tetanus
Infection
Gangrene.

BAB: Will Not Survive.

CHRISTY: Will Not Survive.

MAGGIE: Will Not Survive.

They collapse, exhausted.

* * *

BAB: Day off.

CHRISTY: At last!

BAB: Finally.

MAGGIE: What shall we do?

BAB: Tend to the garden. You?

CHRISTY: Go shopping in town. You?

MAGGIE: Go for a swim.

ALL: A swim?

BAB: Where?

MAGGIE: In the ocean, of course! Grab a towel. I'll steal some sandwiches and a flask of wine.

CHRISTY: Wine? Isn't that, I don't know . . .

BAB: Wonderful?

* * *

They hum "Edith Cavell" as they make their way to the beach.

CHRISTY: There's a long arm of beach south of Pointe du Touquet.

MAGGIE: The sand as soft as Winnipeg Beach.

BAB: The ocean as brooding as Esquimalt's sea.

CHRISTY: The view so far, I can only imagine the Grand River in the distance.

MAGGIE: The water's chilly in May.

CHRISTY: But it's so hot outside!

BAB: Good for cooling off.

They remove their veils and shoes.

They wade into the water.

CHRISTY: *(delighted)* Oooo!

MAGGIE: Well?

CHRISTY: So, so nice.

BAB: Hard to imagine the front just a few hours away.

CHRISTY: And Jack so close, up in England.

BAB: You and him serious?

CHRISTY: Well . . .

MAGGIE: Engaged?

CHRISTY: Well . . .

BAB: Decide on a day?

CHRISTY: Well, the thing is . . . I can't tell you.

MAGGIE: Tell us what?

BAB: *(scandalously)* Secrets!

CHRISTY: Shush.

BAB: Come on!

MAGGIE: Now, now. We all have secrets, and a right to keep them.

CHRISTY *is fraught.*

CHRISTY: Do you promise not to tell?

BAB: Cross our hearts!

CHRISTY: Promise!

MAGGIE: But not to die.

BAB: And I don't want a needle in my eye, either.

CHRISTY: Promise!

MAGGIE: *(laughs)* All right, we promise!

CHRISTY hesitates, then:

CHRISTY: We're already married.

BAB: WHAT?

MAGGIE: How did this come about?

CHRISTY: Jack says: "Let's get married, Christy."
"We can't," I say. "Or I can't join up. It's against the rules."
"We just don't tell anybody until the war's over," he says.
"Only be a coupla months. It'll give us hope," he says.
"Something to see us through."

BAB: Sounds like he said a lot.

MAGGIE: *(a scold)* Bab.

CHRISTY: Got the old priest at the Anglican church in Brantford to do it. Had two friends from high school for witnesses and swore them to secrecy. Didn't even tell our parents.

MAGGIE: How romantic!

BAB: Love is alive! Wait. When did you enlist?

CHRISTY: Two hours after we got married!

BAB: And you were sent to France when?

CHRISTY: Day after we enlisted. "Need nurses right away!"

BAB: But how . . . when did you, you know . . .

MAGGIE: *(warning)* Bab . . .

BAB: I'm just asking.

CHRISTY: When did we what?

BAB: You know.
Con-sum-mate.
The marriage!

CHRISTY: We only had two hours!

BAB: So you got married and you didn't even—

MAGGIE: *(laughing but stern)* Bab!

CHRISTY: What's so funny?

BAB: Did you kiss at least?

CHRISTY: Oh yes, plenty of that.

The other two laugh louder.

You won't tell the matron, will you?

BAB: *(teasing)* Well . . .

MAGGIE: I don't know . . .

BAB: What's in it for us?

CHRISTY: If she finds out, I'll be sent home!

MAGGIE: And you don't want to go home?

CHRISTY: *(honestly)* I don't know. I like who I am here. And I could see things, you know? The world.

MAGGIE: Aye.

CHRISTY: What about you, Bab?

BAB: What about me?

CHRISTY: Is there a man in your life?

BAB: I've fallen in love with a dozen perfectly wonderful soldiers here. And that was only last week.

MAGGIE: Ha!

BAB: I wish I could gather them all up in my lap and hug the whole lot of them.

CHRISTY: Sounds like you'd rather be a mother than a wife.

BAB: Maybe. I wanted to marry a long time ago. But no one seemed to notice. And now I'm getting too old to catch a man's eye.

MAGGIE: I don't know. I've seen that Captain Roberts watching you all week!

BAB: Hush now.

CHRISTY: It's true! He sees you come into the mess, doesn't matter who he's talking to, his eyes never leave you.

BAB: Stop it, both of you!

CHRISTY: Come now, Bab. You've got an eye for the captain as well.

BAB: He *is* very . . .

CHRISTY: Handsome!

MAGGIE: Smart.

CHRISTY: Good with his hands.

> *They look at her.*

In *surgery.*

BAB: YES, yes, you're right. The feeling *is* mutual. Something about men like that makes me crazy.

MAGGIE: What kind of man is that?

BAB: Number one: older.

MAGGIE: Not a bad thing.

BAB: Number two: married.

CHRISTY: Uh oh.

BAB: Exactly.

MAGGIE: You never know.

BAB: I don't think so.

MAGGIE: Things happen. People change.

BAB: Fact is, I can't get to sleep for thinking of him. I just want him all the time. I try my hardest not to. But . . .

CHRISTY: Your secret is safe with us, Bab.

BAB: Thank you, Christy.

They make their way to land. Towel their hair.

MAGGIE: Wine?

BAB: Yes, please.

CHRISTY: I, I shouldn't.

MAGGIE: And why not?

CHRISTY: I've only drank wine in church.

BAB: That's a shame.

CHRISTY: But it is Sunday after all.

MAGGIE: That it is.

CHRISTY: All right, but just a little.

BAB: A toast! To wine!

MAGGIE & CHRISTY: To wine!

They swig and pass the bottle. No glasses here.

BAB: What about you, Maggie?

MAGGIE: What about me?

CHRISTY: Do *you* have a secret?

MAGGIE: Me?

BAB: *(a joke)* Are *you* secretly married?

MAGGIE: Ha. I don't mind men. I like tending to them. But marriage . . . that means *living* with one of them. Being with them *all the time.* No thank you.

CHRISTY: But you like living with women.

MAGGIE: I beg your pardon?

CHRISTY: You roomed with a gal in nursing school—you told me.

MAGGIE: Didn't we all?

CHRISTY: I didn't.

BAB: I lived at home.

MAGGIE: What I mean is . . .

CHRISTY: Even if I did, I'm not sure I'd write to them every day.

MAGGIE: I don't write her *every* day.

CHRISTY: That's not what you told me.

BAB: *(catching on)* . . . Christy.

CHRISTY: What?

BAB: It's none of our business.

CHRISTY: I was just saying . . .

MAGGIE: No.

BAB: What?

MAGGIE: Christy's right.

CHRISTY: I am? About what?

MAGGIE: I do write her. Every day.

BAB: *(careful)* That's nice.

MAGGIE: She's a friend, a close friend.

BAB: *(delicate)* That's good. To have a close friend.

MAGGIE: Her name is . . . Annie.

CHRISTY: I love that name. I think it's a *perfect* name. "Annie."

BAB: *(with caring)* You can trust us, Maggie. Can't she, Christy?

CHRISTY: Of course.

MAGGIE: *(relieved)* Thank you.

CHRISTY: It's nice, isn't it? For us three to trust each other. I feel closer to you both than I do to Jack.

MAGGIE: What a lovely thing to say.

CHRISTY: Friends are for life.

(sudden) I know, I know! Let's make . . . a vow!

BAB: Ha!

MAGGIE: Aren't we too old for vows?

CHRISTY: Never! Come on, come on!

> *CHRISTY creates a seal for them. Perhaps something with spit and palms.*

We shall keep each other's secrets. For all time! Come on, like you mean it!

> *And they do mean it:*

ALL: We shall keep each other's secrets. For all time!

> *They start putting on their shoes and adjusting their clothes. They sing softly under their breath at first, then with gathering energy.*

BAB: "Remember how she gladly nursed your pals, boys . . . Remember how she strived to make them well.

MAGGIE: "Don't forget how patiently she suffered

CHRISTY: "And remember how she bore the prison cell

ALL: "Remember how she bravely gave her life, boys

BAB: "Remember when you're facing shot and shell!

MAGGIE: "She was made of British stuff.

CHRISTY: "So are you, and that's enough!

ALL: "The Bull Dog's loose! Remember Nurse Cavell!"

They are dressed.

BAB: Wait! Picture!

MAGGIE: No!

CHRISTY: You can see my knees!

MAGGIE and CHRISTY protest. But BAB snaps it anyway.

BAB: Nowadays they call that "a candid."

* * *

The whistle sounds.

It carries less anxiety now.

Professional but routine.

BAB: Immediate Care

CHRISTY: Likely to Live

MAGGIE: Will Not Survive.

BAB: Immediate Care

CHRISTY: Likely to Live

MAGGIE: Will Not Survive.

> *They repeat as necessary.*

* * *

CHRISTY: Dear Jack . . .

BAB: Writing to your *hus-band*?

CHRISTY: Shush now.

BAB: Well?

CHRISTY: *(sighs)* I don't know what to say. Jack's letters are so boring. If he ever wrote a real love letter I'd have him examined by a heart specialist. It's like getting letters from a brother.

BAB: Trouble in paradise?

CHRISTY: He wants the life back in Brantford. You know, where I'm a wife and mother. I'm not sure I want that. Everything's different now. I could nurse anywhere. I could do anything.

MAGGIE: Dear Annie. I can imagine the ice breaking on the Assiniboine and the warm winds coming up from the Dakotas.

CHRISTY: Dear Jack . . . *(she stalls)*

MAGGIE: I wish I was there. Taking our nightly walks. Peering into the windows of those red-brick homes by the river. Peeking past the window boxes so carefully watered. Spying on the respectable families dining on their pickerel and turnips. Pretending you and I are those people. Normal.

CHRISTY: Dear Jack . . . *(she stalls)*

BAB: Oh, Grandpa. You said the sea could hold secrets. So here goes.

He asked me to meet him. Captain Roberts. Behind the church in town. After lights out.

I went. It was wonderful. I know it's terrible, but I don't want to have regrets. I could be dead in the morning.

CHRISTY: Dear Jack . . . all's well here. Will write more next week.

She considers, then:

Yours, Christy.

CHRISTY: Apples!

BAB: Beautiful red apples!

MAGGIE: A whole box!

BAB: From British Columbia.

MAGGIE: The rough feel of it in your hand.

CHRISTY: The smell! Like . . . perfume.

BAB: The shiny skin like sun on water.

MAGGIE: After all the mud . . .

BAB: And rain . . .

CHRISTY: . . . And bland mess food . . .

BAB: It's like we have a piece of . . .

ALL: Home.

BAB: Enough apples for every patient.

CHRISTY: Gave one to James, one of the older soldiers—twenty-five, twenty-six maybe? He enlisted four years ago. And he is still alive. A miracle.

BAB: Gave one to Mike while dressing his stump. He said to me:

"Had I known, sister, I would have tried to get myself killed rather than live as a . . . "

MAGGIE: A cripple?

BAB: He dreads going home.

MAGGIE: Gave one to Frank—he's got shell shock. His hands were shaking so hard he couldn't hold it. So I pared it for him. Fed him the pieces slice by slice. Closed his eyes to enjoy it. The way the juice slipped down his dry lips . . .

BAB: Gave one to a boy who . . .

MAGGIE: What?

BAB: (careful) May have caused his own injury.

MAGGIE: Ach.

CHRISTY: Doctor's call them "malingerers." And an English nurse called them "lead swingers." Why don't we just call them cowards?

BAB: I don't like that word.

CHRISTY: But that's what they are, aren't they?

MAGGIE: Medically, they are soldiers with S.I.W.

BAB: What's that?

MAGGIE: "Self-Inflicted Wounds." They are to be considered "undeserving of sympathy or priority in care."

CHRISTY: See?

BAB: I don't know how I feel about that.

CHRISTY: Anger, that's what. All those other boys risking their lives while these fellas . . .

MAGGIE: Not that simple.

BAB: How do you mean?

MAGGIE: I cared for a lad: Leonard. Left his dressing to the last as I was ordered.

Listened to him. Called to a firing line, he was. To execute a soldier for cowardice. The ones shot at dawn. It was his mate. A childhood friend. Not only was he killing the Huns, now he was killing his friends.

He couldn't do it. Shot himself instead, but only managed to graze his own head. And now he's here.

He couldn't kill a friend.

I gave him a sleeping draught, and he had a dreamless sleep till daylight. It was the least I could do.

CHRISTY: They'll send him back into the line right away, I suppose.

MAGGIE: He won't be allowed back to the front. He'll be lucky if he isn't court-martialled and shot for desertion himself.

CHRISTY: *(doubting)* But . . . that doesn't make any sense.

BAB: It doesn't. Does it?

The whistle.

MAGGIE: Enough of this. There's work to do.

* * *

CHRISTY: Three hundred men.

BAB: Burned.

MAGGIE: The German's have a new gas.

CHRISTY: As if the old one wasn't bad enough.

MAGGIE: Symptoms?

BAB: Burning through the pulmonary mucous membrane.

CHRISTY: Profuse excretion from the lacrimal glands.

BAB: Signs of bronchitis or pneumonia.

MAGGIE: Treatment?

CHRISTY: Remove damaged tissue?

BAB: Irrigation.

CHRISTY: Reapply sterile dressings.

MAGGIE: Report:

CHRISTY: Blistered from his neck to his toes on the left side. Took one hour just to do this dressing.

MAGGIE: Report:

BAB: A sister made contact with the gas as she was caring for him. Now she needs treatment herself.

CHRISTY: Now they're coming after us.

MAGGIE: Use rubber gloves and keep a basin of soda water nearby as standard practice.

* * *

MAGGIE: New order from the matron.

BAB: What is it?

MAGGIE: Something new. "Blood transfusion." A direct flow of blood by syringe from a donor to a patient.

BAB: What?

CHRISTY: Sounds dangerous.

MAGGIE: It could save lives.

BAB: *(bitterly)* Anything to get the boys back into battle, right?

* * *

MAGGIE *hands out tubes.*

CHRISTY: What's this?

MAGGIE: Morphine. Carry an extra tube at all times.

BAB: What now?

MAGGIE: Better to take an overdose than be captured by the Germans.

* * *

Once again, the alarm sounds.

CHRISTY: Two a.m.

BAB: Night duty.

MAGGIE: Almost every night now.

CHRISTY: We hear them in the distance.

MAGGIE: "Lights out, please!"

BAB: The drone of the machines overhead.

MAGGIE: *(menacing)* Muuuh, muuuh, muuuh.

BAB: And the anti-aircraft guns.

CHRISTY: *(mimics the sound)* Boom, boom, boom.

BAB: The men trying to sleep.

CHRISTY: It makes me heart sick—that sound.

BAB: German airmen have dropped notes. Announcing their intention to bomb hospitals.

CHRISTY: They wouldn't bomb hospitals, would they?

BAB: They invented chlorine gas, why not bomb hospitals.

CHRISTY: "Cast your cares upon the Lord and he will sustain you. Cast your cares upon . . . "

> *Christy continues under.*

MAGGIE: Matron had a meeting with the military yesterday. Requested helmets for the nurses.

BAB: *(as a man)* "We'll consider it."

MAGGIE: *(as a man)* "Your rank comes with risk, sister-soldier."

BAB: *(as a man)* "It's a war, you know, not a tea party."

CHRISTY: " . . . Cast your cares upon the Lord and he will sustain you . . . "

BAB: We know it's not a party.

MAGGIE: We see more of it than you.

BAB: Mike calls out: "Sister! Help!" Pitch black, I make my way over. Blood pouring from his amputated arm. With one hand, I stop the hemorrhage from the artery. With the other, I bandage and dress the wound. All this in total dark.

MAGGIE: Muuuh, muuuh, muuuh—

BAB: Boom, boom, boom—

CHRISTY: "Cast your cares upon . . . "

MAGGIE: Muuuh, muuuh, muuuh—

BAB: Boom, boom, boom.

CHRISTY: "Cast your—"

MAGGIE: Muuuh, muuuh, muuuh—

CHRISTY: Stop it! Stop It!

Silence.

Then:

They sound the "all-clear."

MAGGIE: What's to be, will be. Being in a bed or in the dugout makes no difference.

CHRISTY: *(calming herself)* It's nothing compared to what the boys are going through. Nothing.

BAB: Nothing to be done. Remind yourself that with every passing day we are the ones still . . .

CHRISTY: Alive.

BAB: Alive.

MAGGIE: Aye. Alive.

* * *

CHRISTY: Day off!

BAB: Finally.

MAGGIE: What shall we do?

ALL: Swim!

* * *

The beach. They hum a tune as they make their way.

They've had their swim.

They towel their hair.

BAB: I figure, if the war ends soon that is, I'd be going home with a thousand dollars in savings plus six months' pay to come.

CHRISTY: What will you do?

BAB: Invest it in the markets.

CHRISTY: To what end?

MAGGIE: She'll have more money.

BAB: Not just money. Freedom.

CHRISTY: Makes sense. We can't be nurses forever.

MAGGIE: Why not? I'd be happy to be head matron at a big hospital. Get up in the morning, go to work, care for people, then go home at night with a cuppa and a book.

CHRISTY: My mother is worried the war will harden my "feminine sensibilities." That I won't be fit for marriage when I get home.

MAGGIE: Little does she know.

BAB: And does she know you were given the vote here? If you can decide on your MP, you can decide on the life you want to live.

CHRISTY: My mother wouldn't vote even if I was the one running. "It's none of our business!"

MAGGIE: They opened the gate with us. No way they'll get that horse back in the barn. First Canadian women ever to vote: Nursing Sisters of the CAMC. Wine?

They pass it along with bread and cheese.

I see Captain Roberts is spending every meal at your table.

BAB: He is, isn't he?

CHRISTY: Come on, Bab, tell us!

BAB: *(mocking)* It's our responsibility to reassure the military that we'll still be suitable daughters, sisters, and wives after the war.

CHRISTY: Ha!

MAGGIE: Och!

BAB: *(mocking)* It's by our social actions that we stand or fall in these men's estimations.

MAGGIE: You're *not* going to tell us, are you?

CHRISTY: Bab! If you can't tell us, who can you tell?

BAB: My dead grandpa, that's who. And the waves.

CHRISTY: That's no fun!

BAB: We've been meeting. After hours. That's all I'll say.

MAGGIE: *(as a man)* "Scandalous!"

CHRISTY: *(as a man)* "Shocking!"

MAGGIE: *(as a man)* "Shameful!"

BAB: And what about *you*? I hear your *hus-band* is coming through on the way to join his unit.

CHRISTY: . . . He is.

MAGGIE: You are less than enthusiastic.

CHRISTY: Nervous, I guess.

BAB: *(teasing)* Will you, you know . . . ?

MAGGIE: *(teasing)* Should we arrange to be "away" from our tent?

CHRISTY: *(embarrassed, loudly)* I don't want to talk about it!

BAB: And how is Annie?

MAGGIE: She thinks she'll be deployed soon.

CHRISTY: How exciting!

BAB: Here?

MAGGIE: Not sure.

CHRISTY: But you hope so.

MAGGIE: I suppose.

BAB: You *suppose?*

MAGGIE: Fine, it would be . . . *wonderful.*

The others laugh.

They drink.

Matron's given us new instructions.

BAB: Ugh.

CHRISTY: What now?

MAGGIE: We are to throw a party for the male officers next week.

CHRISTY: Fun!

BAB: Really? Why can't they throw their own party?

MAGGIE: Being a good nurse isn't going to get you promoted. We need to talk to people.

BAB: Men, you mean.

CHRISTY: I like parties! Besides, it will give us a chance to look at
. . . the landscape.

BAB: You are MARRIED!

CHRISTY: Exactly! It means I can only look! And the CAPTAIN, Bab.
The captain will be there!

BAB: Oh hush!

CHRISTY: What kind of party?

MAGGIE: I don't think it matters. Ideas?

CHRISTY: A picnic, of course.

CHRISTY loves it:

We'll take the officers into the woods. On bikes. Then, we'll have a
lunch of . . . chicken salad?

MAGGIE: Devilled eggs.

BAB: Fruit, please.

MAGGIE: Cakes.

BAB: Tea and lime juice.

CHRISTY: And then AFTER, we'll stroll through the woods, play cards
and such, and when the sun starts to set . . .

BAB: What then, social organizer?

MAGGIE: Wine, I hope.

CHRISTY: And dancing!

CHRISTY gets them up and they take turns dancing with each other as they sing:

"There are many flags waving
Over land and over seas
Though shot and shell are flying
Canada, I think of thee

BAB: "It's the land I'd do or die for
And my heart is there always

MAGGIE: "So when I get back home once more
'Tis there I'll end my days

ALL: "I love you, Canada
For you mean so much to me
I love your hills and valleys
And your stately maple tree
I love all your dear people
Though far away I roam
When I hear them speak of Canada
I long for home sweet home . . . "

They are pretty drunk by now.

MAGGIE: Ah!

CHRISTY: Oh no!

BAB mimics an injury.

BAB: I've got a blighty! Help, sister!

They fall on the ground laughing their heads off.

Dusk descends and the twinkle of a few stars appear.

They gaze up at them.

CHRISTY: I don't want to go home.

MAGGIE: It's good to feel important, isn't it?

BAB: To make a difference.

CHRISTY: Who wants to sit at home and make babies?

MAGGIE: I say "move it over there" and they move it over there.

BAB: I *feel* like a soldier.

CHRISTY: But when I get home . . . I can hear my mother already:

BAB: *(mocking)* "A woman's place is in the home!"

MAGGIE: *(mocking)* "You can be a wife, a teacher, or a nun."

BAB: *(mocking)* "No man will have a nurse for a wife."

MAGGIE: I'll take a hospital position.

BAB: I'll go for private practice, I suppose.

CHRISTY: What other choice do I have?

BAB: I'm not sure who I am anymore outside of this.

CHRISTY: Or who I'd *want* to be.

MAGGIE: It's silly. We live in this world devoted to men. And yet we spend most of our time with each other. Sisters. Why do we always talk about them? Why don't we talk more about us? Why don't we defend each other?

BAB sits up.

BAB: Let's make another vow.

CHRISTY: Yes! Yes!

They seal the vow as:

MAGGIE: We will defend each other to the end.

ALL: To the end!

MAGGIE: And maybe . . . beyond.

* * *

The whistle.

They go through the motions, rote/machine-like:

MAGGIE: Tetanus.

BAB: Infection.

CHRISTY: Gangrene.

MAGGIE: Tetanus.

BAB: Infection.

CHRISTY: Gangrene.

Repeat as necessary.

* * *

BAB: Bennett, my brain case, died last night. So glad he is out of his suffering.

CHRISTY: Steven's shrapnel moved into his lungs. I hope he finds peace soon.

MAGGIE: Discharged Frank today. Shell shock wasn't getting better, so home he goes. "Thanks, sister," he said, but there were tears streaming down his face.

CHRISTY: Michael will do anything to not get discharged: mend leaky milk pails, tea urns, buckets.

BAB: Bill, he'd been at the front for months. I didn't play fair. Made a wrong register on his chart.

MAGGIE: James—he's too ill to go back to the front. And he's been in France for four years! I placed his thermometer onto a hot water bottle before putting it into his mouth.

"Yes, much too ill," . . . says the doctor. I hope he gets back home to Saskatchewan soon.

BAB: New doctor yesterday. He was marking up too many men for the front.

"A big battle and they need men," . . . he says.

"They need cannon fodder," I thought.

I told the matron. He was transferred this morning.

CHRISTY: I had a German POW on my ward last night.

BAB: A Hun? What did you do?

CHRISTY: I looked down the row of our wounded boys and thought: "I can't do it, Matron. Nurse a Hun?"

BAB: What did she say?

CHRISTY: "Sister, he's only a boy."

MAGGIE: We are obligated to treat them as well.

CHRISTY: I looked at him. The boy. His guts had been blown out by shrapnel. He wouldn't make it through the night. His name was Franz.

"*Bitte*," he says. "*Bitte*."

He was scared. A wounded boy without a friend on any side.

I read a verse to him: "Do not be afraid, for I am with you; do not be dismayed, for I am your God. I will strengthen you and help you."

I slipped my arm under his head to give him a drink of water, and he looked up into my face. He caught my hand and kissed it. Then he was gone.

I kept thinking about his mother in Germany. I wished she could know that someone had been with her little boy at the last. That he wasn't alone.

MAGGIE: That was good, Christy, what you did.

BAB: And yet, that boy's overlords keep threatening to bomb us.

MAGGIE: Bab!

BAB: It's true. They bomb us, we bomb them, they kill us, we kill them, we sew them up and send them back for more bombing and killing.

I'm so . . . *sick* of the suffering. Every *day* . . . every *day*. To go on duty, only to see . . . those boys, those BOYS, marching their way to be wrecked. BOYS.

I can't bear it. I can't. I mean, *what are we actually doing here?*

* * *

MAGGIE: Will Not Survive.

* * *

BAB: What's wrong?

CHRISTY: Jack. He was here for two days. We hadn't seen each other in six months.

BAB: And?

CHRISTY: He was different. He'd never seen me in my uniform. He . . . *saluted* me. "Hello, Lieutenant."

BAB: A joke, surely?

CHRISTY: Didn't feel that way.

And then, because I outranked him, and because they don't know we are married, Matron wouldn't let us eat together, or even socialize.

We didn't even have a moment to . . . kiss or . . .

And the next day, he was off to the front.

I don't know how I feel. I don't know if I can . . . Oh God, Bab, I don't know what to do!

* * *

BAB: Will Not Survive.

* * *

CHRISTY: What's wrong, Maggie?

MAGGIE: It's Annie. She's been dispatched.

CHRISTY: Here?

MAGGIE: Salonika.

Salonika! I'm so worried. What do I tell her? That Greece sounds warm and sunny, but the conditions there are the worst? Excessive heat, lice, lack of water, nurses dying?

CHRISTY: I . . . oh no.

MAGGIE: I keep thinking . . . We were sitting. At the park. By the river. Holding hands. And we talked, about what are lives might be. Together. And then she, she whispered in my ear . . . something I knew was true. But I couldn't . . . my own words got caught in my throat and I . . .

CHRISTY: "Love is patient, Love is kind."

MAGGIE: No. No, it's not. It's easy for you, Christy. You have a choice. You're already married and you don't even want to be. But for Annie and I . . .

CHRISTY: . . . I didn't mean . . .

MAGGIE: Why couldn't I tell her? Why couldn't I say the words? Oh, Annie, be careful!

* * *

CHRISTY: Will Not Survive.

* * *

MAGGIE: What's wrong, Bab?

BAB: I can't . . .

MAGGIE: What?

BAB: No blood. For two months.

MAGGIE: Oh no. Could it be the stress? They've been feeding us less and less.

BAB: No, Maggie. I can feel it. I just know. I can't tell the captain.

MAGGIE: Perhaps not.

BAB: And I can't tell the matron.

MAGGIE: No, that would be bad.

BAB: I can't be rid of it—not here anyway. If they found out, I'd be court-martialled.

MAGGIE: Oh, Bab . . .

BAB: What am I going to do?

* * *

MAGGIE: Here.

CHRISTY: What's this?

MAGGIE: Masks. From the Red Cross.

BAB: What for?

MAGGIE: A new kind of influenza. They're calling it Spanish Flu.

BAB: Why the masks?

MAGGIE: Prevent transmission. Wear one at all times.

CHRISTY: Even on the wards?

MAGGIE: Especially on the wards.

BAB: But they won't see our faces.

MAGGIE: And you won't see theirs either. Make sure each patient gets one too. It is spreading fast. They've admitted 1,400 cases in the last week alone. HQ says it has a twenty-six per cent mortality rate.

BAB: Oh my God.

CHRISTY: How do we treat it?

MAGGIE: Like pneumonia. Lots of liquids. Keep the fever down. Avoid exposure.

BAB: What about the boys we're sending home?

MAGGIE: We're hoping the voyage back will act as a quarantine.

CHRISTY: I do hope they don't take it back with them.

BAB: That would be the real disaster.

MAGGIE: Aye.

* * *

CHRISTY: They die.

MAGGIE: They die.

BAB: Every day.

CHRISTY: So many.

BAB: Unconscious or delirious.

MAGGIE: "Sister," he said. His name was Thomas.

"Please stay with me?"

He knew he was dying.

"Sister, please stay with me?"

Because there was nobody. A new convoy of injured came in, and it was all hands in.

The alarm went up, but I told the matron:

"I won't leave him. He deserves to have someone there when he goes."

The alarm passed, and so did he.

I was docked a day's pay for disobeying. But I just couldn't leave him.

* * *

BAB: Letter to Jack?

CHRISTY: No. I'm writing down the names of every one of my patients who died. I'm writing to the families as well. I try to do ten a night. But I'm sad to say I'm four hundred behind.

Yesterday, I wrote to the family of that German prisoner. I hope they find someone to translate.

MAGGIE: Diary to your grandpa?

BAB: No. Writing to a widow. "Dear Mrs. Sutherland . . . I thought that your husband had slipped into a coma when he said:

'Sister, would you give me my wife's picture? It is in my backpack'

I put your picture in his hand. He lay quietly for a while and then slipped away."

CHRISTY: Letter to Annie?

MAGGIE: No. A boy asked me to write to his mother. I told her he was not alone when he died, nor when he was buried. And that the graves were kept nice. So that his mother might imagine being here herself.

CHRISTY: It's the last chance. For the dead to speak.

BAB: The dead.

MAGGIE: The dead. Aye.

* * *

BAB: I'll say I was secretly married. After I enlisted. And that he's dead.

MAGGIE: And the matron?

BAB: She won't think twice. And even if she did, she wouldn't have time to care.

MAGGIE: And one of those brave boys will have a child.

BAB: No matter boy or girl. And I'll teach them to sail and to catch fish fresh from the sea. And I'll teach them to talk to the waves. Please, Maggie. Talk to the matron? Make her understand? I need to go home.

MAGGIE: Aye. Home.

* * *

MAGGIE: Dearest Annie. I have a plan. Once the war is over, we'll go home. We'll find work. And we'll pick a place on Wolseley Avenue for sale or rent, doesn't matter. We'll live quietly. We'll water our window boxes and stare out over the river. And when we're old, we'll take care of each other.

Because I love you, Annie. I love you. And I'm truly sorry I didn't say it before.

Annie? Can you hear me?

* * *

CHRISTY: Oh God.

BAB: Christy, what's wrong?

CHRISTY: It's Jack, he . . .

She hands BAB *the letter, who reads it out loud.*

BAB: "My dear wife . . .

CHRISTY: . . . Wife . . .

BAB: "I've been injured. Lost both my legs in the battle at . . . "

Oh, Christy. There's nothing you could have done.

CHRISTY: Keep going.

BAB: "I'm on my way back to Brantford. If you tell the matron we're married, they'll let you come home. You'll be taking care of me now, Christy."

CHRISTY: I want to care for people, Bab, I do. But now I'll be a wife and a nurse, and I haven't even . . . I just wanted a little freedom.

She weeps.

Oh God, why did I wish for that? Why did I?

* * *

A deep breath from them all.

Exhaustion.

ALL: Will Not Survive.

* * *

CHRISTY: *(matter of fact)* Day off.

MAGGIE: *(weary)* Day off, aye.

BAB: Swim.

* * *

On the beach.

They are sad and numb.

MAGGIE: Wine?

CHRISTY: No thanks.

BAB: Not today.

CHRISTY: No bread. No hot chocolate. No cakes to be had in town. Not for cash or trade.

They dip their feet in the water.

The hush of the waves.

BAB: Did you hear? Sister Susan's resigned. She's going to marry a patient going home.

MAGGIE: Sister Mary's leaving. Her father's died in Quebec. Her mother needs help taking care of eleven children.

BAB: How do I look? Do I look old? I feel *old*.

MAGGIE: I don't think the bags under my eyes will ever go away.

CHRISTY: I *feel* different. A month here feels like a year back home.

They hum "Here We Are, Here We Are Again" for a moment.

It feels sad.

Today is Whitsunday. Pentecost.

MAGGIE: Is it.

CHRISTY: Shall we go to the service?

BAB: Ugh. Not if it's all doom and gloom . . .

CHRISTY: Come on. The new chaplain's very nice.

BAB: And good-looking too.

MAGGIE: Bab, ya cannae be a Catholic AND good looking.

CHRISTY: Let's go! It'll be good for us! A little faith. Whadya say?

MAGGIE: Sure.

BAB: Of course. Then again . . .

They stare out over the sea.

Who wants to leave this?

MAGGIE: If only airplanes could fly across the ocean. The way blue-birds migrate from Mexico to Manitoba. I'd fly back home by the time the maple trees in Winnipeg turn red.

BAB: I can't help think that maybe my grandpa's watery bones have followed me here. That he's nearby somehow.

CHRISTY: Odd how water can look the same no matter where you are. If I squint, I'd have thought I was back in Ontario on the edge of Lake Erie.

MAGGIE: Let us make another vow. That every year we meet and have a swim and take in the sunset. Promise?

No ritual this time. Only their deep-hearted commitment.

CHRISTY: Yes. I promise.

BAB: I promise.

CHRISTY: Take another picture, Bab. Please?

BAB does, but the pose is one of reflection and sadness.

* * *

CHRISTY: Sunday.

BAB: May 18.

MAGGIE: 1918.

BAB: Evening.

CHRISTY: Whitsunday.

MAGGIE: Pentecost.

CHRISTY: Apostles, chapter two, verse one: "And lo, when that day came, they were all together in one place."

BAB: We're coming back from the evening service.

MAGGIE: Walking back to our tent.

BAB: When we hear it.

CHRISTY: "When suddenly a sound like the blowing of a violent wind came from heaven . . . "

BAB: An airplane. But this time so low . . .

MAGGIE: Is it ours?

BAB: The French?

MAGGIE: Never dreaming . . .

BAB: . . . The Huns.

MAGGIE: Oh no.

CHRISTY: "And the sound filled the whole house where they were sitting."

BAB: Our lights all burning.

MAGGIE: When finally—

CHRISTY: "And they saw what seemed to be tongues of fire . . . "

BAB: The alarm!

The alarm.

It begins the same, but rises until it becomes a cry of something deep and horrible within them until:

BAB: Bombs!

CHRISTY: The ward's been struck!

MAGGIE: The oil heaters—overturned!

CHRISTY: Follow the protocols.

MAGGIE: Water! Water!

BAB: Stamp out the fires.

MAGGIE: More water!

Go!

BAB: Move!

MAGGIE: Faster!

CHRISTY: The beds—they're catching fire!

MAGGIE: Oh God.

CHRISTY: The boys! We've got to get them out!

BAB: Christy!

MAGGIE: No!

CHRISTY: "And it separated, and came to rest on each of them."

MAGGIE: Bab! Don't—

CHRISTY: "And they were filled with the Holy Spirit and began to speak in other tongues."

BAB: Maggie!

MAGGIE: Bab? Where are you?

CHRISTY: "Amazed and perplexed, they asked one another:"

ALL: "Oh God, what does this mean?"

An explosion of light and sound.

It exists in their minds, bodies, voices.

It settles.

* * *

The "all-clear" sounds quietly, as if a distant memory.

MAGGIE: *(to BAB)* I saw you dragging out a boy when your clothing caught fire.

BAB: *(to CHRISTY)* I saw you rushing back in the building just as a fresh bomb shattered the windows.

CHRISTY: *(to MAGGIE)* I saw you sinking into the mud, strafed with machine gun fire from above.

MAGGIE: We were a direct target.

CHRISTY: A hospital.

BAB: A hospital.

MAGGIE: A hospital, aye.

* * *

These are facts and retold with pride and professionalism:

CHRISTY: I was the first to die.

BAB: Then I.

MAGGIE: Then I.

They slowly begin to remove their uniforms. Their undergarments are now red with injury.

CHRISTY: Shrapnel. My femoral artery severed. Died from shock. Didn't take long.

MAGGIE: It was a beautiful funeral. A Tuesday. Your grave lined with white and purple lilacs and pink peonies. One hundred and ten Canadian Sisters followed in procession, with English, even American officers, marching down the road from the hospital to the Étaples graveyard. Funny, the chaplain and I had just been the week before to lay flowers and say a prayer.

CHRISTY: Oh, Jack, we were so young. You were my only love, I promise.

BAB: I was next. Fever for three days. A wounded leg and fractured femur. But the burns were the worst. All I wanted was water. Cool, cold Canadian water. And then it was over.

CHRISTY: The sisters and officers made another walk to Étaples. The sun was warm, and the birds were singing. Your coffin was draped with a flag, your uniform veil, and your belt. Representing all of who you are: Canadian. Woman. Nurse. Soldier.

BAB: I'm like you now, Grandpa. Our memories both swallowed by time. But with no child to carry them forward.

MAGGIE: I went last. Ten days after the attack. I'd been unconscious the whole time. Shrapnel had torn me apart: skin, skull, chest. What else does a person have worth keeping?

BAB: A blistering hot day, yours. The sisters always went. Couldn't stand the thought of us going without a woman close by.

MAGGIE: Ach, Annie. I never thought I'd be saying goodbye so soon.

* * *

BAB: Look.

The photos appear. Perhaps they are translucent, developing in front of our eyes.

It's us. It's us.

The women see themselves now, when they were living.

And now, a revelation.

BAB: We are the dead. Aren't we?

CHRISTY: Are we?

MAGGIE: Aye. We are the dead.

* * *

Darkness descends.

BAB: Swim?

CHRISTY: Yes.

MAGGIE: Aye, swim.

* * *

They sing softly as they step into the water.

BAB: "Here we are . . .

MAGGIE: "Here we are . . .

CHRISTY: "Here we are again . . .

BAB: "There's Pat and Mac and Bonnie and Jack and Jo.

MAGGIE: "Never mind the weather . . .

CHRISTY: "Now we're all together . . .

ALL: "Hallo, hallo, here we are again!"

They float.

BAB: Next year?

MAGGIE: Aye. And always.

CHRISTY: We made a vow.

They stare up at the sky.

BAB: Such a clear night.

MAGGIE: Like you can see the whole universe. From one end to the other.

CHRISTY: "And I will bless thee
And I will multiply thy descendants
As the stars of heaven
And as the sand . . .
Which lies upon the shore."

They float.

As the sea . . .
. . . washes their injuries clean.

End of play.

AFTERWORD

Some years ago, I visited the Vimy Ridge memorial in France. I had been there twice before, but this time my wife Susie was along for the journey. We were led by my friend and colleague, Simon Godly, an expert in WWI battlefields. Simon had assisted me with research on both *Vimy* and *Einstein's Gift*, both dealing with the horrors of the First World War. Susie asked him a question he is rarely asked: "Where are all the women?"

Simon took us to Boulogne-sur-Mer. There at the Wimereux Communal Cemetery, at least ten women were buried. Simon confirmed that Boulogne-sur-Mer and nearby Étaples were hospital sites, often called "Hospital City" at the time. Simon also showed us the Étaples graveyard, a magnificent, overwhelming thing to behold, where the three women in this play lay buried.

On May 19, 1918, No. 1 Canadian General Hospital near Étaples was attacked by air. Katherine Macdonald, Margaret Lowe, and Gladys Wake lost their lives.

I began to piece together, in my imagination and also based on research, something of a life for each of these women. This is one of my callings as a dramatist: to create characters, to resurrect lives forgotten, to make them live again for a short time, in front of an audience in the present. As I did in writing *Vimy*, I wanted to connect each character with their sense of home and geography.

Even today, the bombing of hospitals and other civilian sites is not uncommon. These horrors are brought to us continually via both traditional and social media. Sadly, the lives of these women, who we now call "front-line workers" or "first responders" are an even more important reminder of the universal and timeless tragedy and ruthlessness of war.

Canadian nurses were nicknamed "Bluebirds" because of their blue dresses, accented by white aprons and sheer veils. Real-life bluebirds can be found across Canada today in emergency rooms, ambulances, and as soldiers of our military.

Bless these women for their daring, sense of adventure, sacrifice, and love for their fellow humans. If you are ever in France, pay them a visit, won't you?

I am deeply indebted to the following individuals and organizations: Natasha MacLellan, Artistic Director of TNB, for believing in this play from the start. Thanks to all the actors who did workshops of this play, virtual productions during the pandemic, and those who performed in a short version of this play previously published. Thanks to Louise Casemore, who dramaturged this play, and Susie Moloney who read every draft. Thanks to Theatre Alberta, and to the Artstrek program for commissioning the idea in the first place. The Canada Council and Alberta Foundation for the Arts assisted in the writing of the play. Rebecca, Don, and Amy, thanks for keeping the flame going.

A special thanks to Cynthia Toman. Her landmark work *Sister Soldiers* is the definitive record of these women. I could not have written the play without her research, guidance, and generosity.

—Vern Thiessen
Winnipeg 2022

Vern Thiessen is one of Canada's most produced playwrights. His plays have been translated into five languages and have been seen around the world. Vern is the recipient of the Dora Mavor Moore and Elizabeth Sterling Haynes awards for Outstanding New Play, the Carol Bolt Award, the Gwen Pharis Ringwood Award, and the Governor General's Literary Award for Drama, Canada's highest honour for a playwright. He has served as president of both the Playwrights Guild of Canada and the Writers Guild of Alberta and was artistic director of Workshop West Playwrights' Theatre for six seasons. He is married to acclaimed screen-writer and novelist Susie Moloney.